The Human Villager.

Edgar Antonio Vargas Figuera.

INDEX:

In honor of why I exist:

My God.

My Mother: Merari Del Carmen Figuera Pérez.

My Father: Pedro Antonio Vargas Pérez.

My Daughters: Yennis Carolina Rodríguez.

Edlin Michell Vargas Ortiz.

Lined de los Ángeles Vargas Ortiz.

Arelis Patricia Marín.

My Children's: Leonardo Antonio Vargas Ortiz.

Edgar Antonio Vargas Gimon.

My Granddaughters and My Grandchildren.

Chapter I
The Prelude.

Along the road adjacent to the mountain, a man walked slowly looking for a path that would take him to the top. In the city he had heard that several long-lived families made the decision to found a community on the plateau of that hill. This story woke up in the character a mental concern that every day gained more strength, he wanted to know why these people decided to live away from the cosmopolitan metropolis, a place where they had lived a lifetime with their already formed family.

Going up the slope along the path found, he began to observe the flora and fauna with an extraordinary diversity, gradually, the climate changed from warm to cold, the vegetation was more dense, the trees showed their autumnal majesty, on them the primates moved by jumping through the branches, they did not leave one while they secured the other, they issued an alert sound, or perhaps, it seemed that they welcomed the walker, on the other hand, some birds took up their flight and others sang eagerly, a rhythm of melodies that reached the ear of the visitor as if it were a concert of **Love and Peace**.

From that moment the man began to feel that spiritual joy within his soul, he had walked a considerable distance, something exhausted sought support in a root that sprouted from the earth, that root was from a very old tree, sitting on it he turned his gaze several times in 180º, I only saw the path that was once trodden by many people, now the dense vegetation little by little was recovering what one day was taken from it, that's nature, at the time she rightly claims what was given to her corresponds.

After cooling down, the man resumed his march, a deep breath filled his spirit to reach the place whose adventure had been proposed, after walking for a prudent time, he observed a kind of road that came from the east to the west, it looked like a belt that It bordered the hill, even when its width denounced it, no traces of vehicular traffic were observed, the road was worked with landscaping criteria, on carved stones they preserved the slope of the mountain, only a small cut was made to be able to transit, this work of engineering caught the attention of the adventurer, walking for a while observing the thick vegetation on both sides of the road, sharpening his senses he was able to conclude that the road, apart from serving people to travel, was equally valid as a firebreak at the time of a forest fire, in this case nature could understand such an action, since it was justified because it was part of its own protection.

A cloud of dust in the distance and the noise of an engine caught the attention of the walker, he discreetly took a malicious protective measure, when the unexpected visitor approached he observed two people riding a motorcycle, the mutual reception was very affectionate, dispelling any concerns out of the ordinary, immediately a small routine dialogue originated:

- Are you on an adventure friend?
- Something similar. The walker replied.
- Can we help you with something?

- I come to visit a community called **"The Prelude".**
- My friend, on the other side of the mountain there are cars that could have taken him.
- That's what they told me, but I preferred to go up the path, to live the adventure of the people who founded that community.
- Good! He still has a way to go. Do you want Juan to accompany you?
- Do you live in that community?
- We are grandchildren of the founders.
- ¡Excellent!

Around noon, the hiker with his companion began to see the plateau of the hill and some people who could not be distinguished very well due to the distance, when they approached they saw a procession of long-lived women with jars full of natural juice and cookies of different flavors, this was the fabulous reception they gave the visiting man. **¡Such was the cordiality of those human people!**

Once installed in a churuata made with wooden pilasters and a palm roof, the amazed man could not believe what his eyes were looking at, a long-lived man of about 75 years, broke the visitor's charm, making the following comment:

- Maria, I think that 10 years ago we did not see a person go up that path.
- I think more. The woman answered.
- Friend, what brought you here?
- In the city they told me the history of this community and it caught my attention to learn how it was founded. I would like someone to tell me that wonderful story.
- Here there is not much to tell, but what you see, however, Pedro is there, he could tell you something.

- Thank you! The truth is, you look like some extraordinary people.

From that day on, a close bond began between the inhabitants of **The prelude and The Walker**.

The hill that these people had chosen to live, was the highest that belonged to the eastern mountain range of a country called Venezuela, with an approximate altitude of 1,800 meters above sea level, the top of the mountain allowed a panoramic view that rotated in a total circumference, to the north you could see the reflection of the blue sky blending with the waters of the Caribbean Sea, thus provoking the sensation of an infinite horizon, to the south the dammed waters of the rivers created an immense freshwater lake, from east to west, exuberant vegetation oxygenated all that marvelous territory.

Most of the people that made up this citadel were academic professionals who risked breaking the paradigm of a utopia created by contemporary society, in the same way that artisans, cultivators, artists were added to that idea and in general, many people flourished. Framed in that human thought, always believing that the spiritual retreat based on the Monolithic Unit of Probos Human Beings, should be directly linked with Nature. Everyone knew that Humanity was made up entirely of Humans, in such a way they knew that **Being**, a Human **Being**, was something dignified and for this reason they wanted to leave the earthly world, with perceptible traces bathed in **Human Dignity.**

This small expression with a high social content, has been demonstrated by history since human existence, even though it is said that the human species appeared in the world more than 200,000 years ago, in the same way there are historical records regarding the intervention of a divine word The human encounter of the tangible with the intangible, has been an obligatory subject to move the synderesis of thought, the trillions of neurons that the human brain contains, have always worked to reach a conclusion that frames Science with the Divine. A natural comparison could be that all the waters of the rivers always reach the sea, it is up to the Human to know **who the Sea is**. For these people it was not difficult to conclude that the sea was the **Divine**, of course, three quarters of the globe is made up of water and it should be noted that the human body likewise has almost the same proportion.

History tells that the Chinese, Egyptian, Mesopotamian, Greek, Roman, Mayan, Aztec and Inca civilizations, in ancient times, had their own belief in the Divine, that is, they had their own gods, although they could never look at them, they created images to worship them. In its own way, now, the engine that moved this belief about something Intangible, could only have a name. **FAITH!** But what is FAITH?

Faith is the belief, confidence or assent of a person in relation to something or someone and, as such, it manifests itself above the need to have evidence that demonstrates the truth of what is believed. The word comes from the Latin fides, which means 'loyalty', 'fidelity'.

In this sense, humans have that intrinsic Faith in their Being, some of them on many occasions have taken advantage of that good Faith, fought in a barbaric way to impose it on others, thus causing misfortunes on entire towns, in the same way, scientific evolution has created lethal artifacts and mechanisms to destroy the human race, when so arranged by any human with **POWER.**

We find this human picture in many places on the globe, those who for pleasures seek **power** to dominate Humanity, however, there are also **Human Beings**, who have fought in the same way for good to prevail, currently Science has understood that a Superior Energy Source coexists within the universe, which has manifested itself through Positive Energy Vibrations between Humans, which in the same way we could call it FAITH!, the purpose of this intangible revelation, is directed to the thinking human so that try to achieve a rearrangement of the big house, which must be directed to the common good of **Humanity.**

It is very likely that the motivation of the people to form the community **"the prelude"** originated from the argument of looking for a place that would allow them to finish living their lives in collective harmony, based on the principle of being people who think about their own **earthly existence**.

A person with pure spiritual knowledge, realizes many things that happen around him, especially when he knows his Virtues, Defects, Weaknesses and Strengths, they will lead him to perform very noble acts, and his existence is in full use of his senses. And mental faculties, at that moment he knows his own **conscience** and begins to appreciate everything he thinks, feels, says, wants or does. Without a doubt, these people will always walk the right path, trying to think and plan their actions, so that other people see and observe where they should walk in life. The basis of our way of acting is closely linked to thoughts and emotions, this activity invites us to self-observe the way in which our body reacts to emotions and which are later reflected in our **actions**.

The awareness of these people with their noble attitudes, led them to think that freedom and tranquility can be achieved, just by being indifferent to material comforts and external fortunes, perhaps, they thought that dedicating themselves to a life guided by the principles of reason and virtue were enough, they had understood that striving in common work would lead them to the goal of the well-being of a life that is worth living, a life in which the maximum potential of the Being is reached with the Human, for this reason it can also be translated as Flowering, that is, that the person has Flowered as a **Human Being.**

These people, as conscious human beings, intervened in the natural purity of that hill, applying all the healthy criteria that science and technology allowed them, using the necessary spaces to incorporate all the services required in an urban planning, in the same way, they were very prudent in looking for a source of energy that would not harm the environment.

Regarding food production, they took advantage of the technology based on controlled cultivation houses to produce vegetables and legumes in the open air, in the same way, they built sheds where they produced broiler chickens, laying hens, pens for ducks, turkeys and geese, as well, a fenced area for raising goats, rams and sheep, small pastures for dual-purpose cows (fattening and milking) and small sheds with their pigpens for raising pigs.

Knowing cause and effect, these people searched for a way to produce their own food system. It is important to understand and understand that the first need of a Human Being is to nourish themselves healthily, for this they must act freely.

For what they could not produce in the community, they created a grocery store, understanding that the grocery store was a supply center for clothing, medicine, tools, food, and objects for daily use; also, a place of sociability where the inhabitants met to talk about political events, gossip and to carry out recreational activities, it was supplied with the surpluses that originated from the aforementioned production, that is, the mentality of these people was sufficiently lucid in taking advantage of all the benefits that nature itself provided, based on physiocratie thought, where its economic doctrine maintains that wealth came exclusively from the exploitation of the natural resources of each organized community and the free exchange of products among themselves , in addition to maintaining the existence of a natural order of **human societies.**

Regarding Health, they built a small dispensary with all the necessary elements for primary care and any emergency that might arise, for knowledge they created a technological communication center, where they could go to investigate any information provided by the advances of the world technology, that is, these people had thought of three basic elements of good living, which are: Food, Health and Education. The other additions arrived on their own, this is part of the spell when people know how to work in Unión Monolithic.

This small citadel that did not exceed 500 homes, was made up of about 2,000 people, including 750 women over 60 years of age and 800 men over 65 years of age, which represented 77.50% of the population, this population percentage could be considered an open-air nursing home, where people could enjoy free recreation in direct contact with Nature, many said that this allowed them to feel fulfilled and extend their earthly life, the other 22.50% were represented by young people who did not reach At age 40, they were prepared to take care of the facilities and direct all food production.

This perfect unity broke the utopia created by human societies, many people thought that humans could not unite in a project of this magnitude, it is very likely that from human to human that would be impossible, but when human beings with clear mentalities are found in solidarity and away from the evil that selfishness produces, of course you can.

How many debates would these people carry out to arrive at such an important conclusion for their earthly life, it is very likely that the egalitarian dialogue is the consequence of valid arguments for their claims of human coexistence and not of creating **individual power.**

The values as principles, allowed them to redirect their personal behavior, to the path of Being, a Human Being, these fundamental beliefs helped them to prefer, appreciate and choose some things instead of others, their ideals became indicators of the path to follow, They allowed them to make sense of what they did, to make the right decisions, to take responsibility for their actions and to accept their consequences. In other words, they allowed them to clearly define the goals of life as Human Beings.

Since the evolution of the human species, humans have understood the need they have for each other, in order to evolve in the world, socialization was the first vital act of earthly coexistence and thus achieve what we now call Humanity, but the Humanity is not only the group of humans, but also the behavior of humans within their own essence, however, their tendency to think and act independently of others, without being subject to general rules of coexistence, in addition to believing that they are autonomous and supremacy in their rights as an individual before society, were the gateway to Individualism.

Individualistic people tend to promote the exercise of their goals, with their own desires and independent of their self-sufficiency, they are totally opposed to external interventions on their own initiatives, be they: social, state, institutional or group. This attitude can be combated, preserving a shared synergy with emerging social groups, always defending a positive attitude, where good humor helps overcome any crisis situation and favors the appropriate changes for the common good of human beings.

Thinking human beings who reason about an organized community, always seek what is convenient for the collective, distinguish the interdependence of its members and encourage the well-being of the group over the individual, that is, the achievement of group objectives over individual ones. The worth of the individual lies in how he contributes to society.

All people have rights in the human world, they are indivisible and interdependent, this means that a set of rights cannot be fully enjoyed without the others, for example, advancing civil and political rights, facilitating the exercise of economic rights , social and cultural, which are inherent to all human beings, regardless of nationality, place of residence, sex, national or ethnic origin, color, religion, language, or any other condition, therefore, everyone has the same human rights, without phobias or discrimination.

Among the multiple characteristics of human rights, the fact that they are progressive and irreversible stands out; that is to say, a new right does not exclude or nullify a previous right. In this sense, the new social conditions produce the expansion of all human rights.

Human rights are:

- **Imprescriptible**, which means that they can never be removed, because they never cease to be valid.
- **Inalienable**, which means that it cannot be assigned to anyone.
- **Inalienable**, because no one can give them up.

Without a doubt, Social influence is present in all areas of human life, society influences the perceptions, attitudes, judgments, opinions and behavior of people, it has an implicit fundamental obligation that is respect for others and the right to enjoy the same real opportunities to advance in the levels of quality of life, which is why every individual modifies their behavior based on the interaction they have with their environment, relating to others helps to understand that it is not about oneself, but about the person with whom we communicate, that helps to understand that, no matter how hard we work, no matter how pleasant we are, we will not get far unless we can work as a team or with others.

The authentic expression that human beings must always maintain is mutual respect and enjoying the same opportunities, when this becomes a reality, it has a sense of absolute truth, this great truth cannot be manipulated and does not depend on the tastes or interests of each person, things are as they are and their knowledge is only true when it adjusts to reality. In this way the truth is not only universal, that is, for everyone, but it is also forever, it is eternal and timeless, it is independent of who formulates it. Likewise, truth is a value linked to honesty and ethics, which implies the attitude of maintaining truthfulness in words and actions at all times.

The truth can be reached only through experience, understanding and reason, consequently, it is a value that gives an ethical sense to the respect that must exist within human relationships, it constitutes one of the basic pillars where moral conscience is based. of the community and encompasses all areas of human life.

Thus, ethics expresses the ultimate end where human beings find happiness, because happiness is the perfect and endless possession of absolute good; and the only absolute good is **God.**

The walking man, after having walked through the entire community, observed a development that complied with all engineering and urban architecture regulations, going to Mr. Pedro's house, it caught his attention that none of the houses had a perimeter fence for protection , the separation from one another, was through a garden composed of beautiful flowers that emitted captivating aromas and which were jealously cared for by the women, a long-lived woman was in charge of receiving the visitor;

- How are you ma'am? I'm looking for Mr. Pedro.
- Toñito! A gentleman is looking for you.
- Come forward mate, I know what you are coming for.
- Thank you! It caught my attention that they still call him Toñito, that's an expression for a child.
- It has become customary to call me that, my first name is Pedro Antonio, the same as my father had, I imagine that my mother began to call me Toñito to differentiate me from my father.
- Excellent deduction. Tell me, Toñito. How did they get here?
- This began a long time ago, when I had already crossed the threshold of 50 years, every afternoon I met with some

friends thinking what we were going to do when the nest was empty, we all agreed to seek a more direct contact with Nature, we were aware that she is a generator of life, therefore, she fills us with life. After multiple meetings that at times seemed like a chimera, one day we firmly made the decision to explore this hill.

- Why did you choose this hill and not another?
- Look at that building in the city that stands out from the others, the tallest.
- I already saw it, the yellow one is the tallest of all.
- Well, on the roof of that building we contemplated this mountain range and we observed that this was the highest hill, we wanted it to be that way to be closer to the stars and that we could contemplate the natural magic that surrounded it.
- They made a good decision, risky, but good.
- We knew about the risks that could arise, but we all have knowledge of things that in the end helped us a lot. When we decided to intervene on the natural top of this hill, our idea was always framed in using the necessary space, but never affecting the elements that nature took so many years to create, as you can see, the trees that did not bear fruit, we replaced them with fruit trees, of course, within the time that she herself gave us.
- I am surprised Toñito, I never thought that fruit trees could be planted on top of a hill.
- We thought so at first, but after several consultations we concluded that a tree only needs fertile soil and its basic nutrients, such as: Nitrogen, Phosphorus and Potassium.
- Toñito, but this hill is full of rocks and stones. How they did?
- Excavations necessary for its adaptability and we fill them with fertile soil obtained right here, do not forget, comrade, that we are in a tropical zone, this environment offers us as a result, being privileged by divine providence, we are all

aware that our intervention is for the common good of many human beings, that means that the hand of God helps us to make it so.

- And boy has it helped them!
- Do you believe in God?
- Of course!
- Then put into practice the virtues of your **Faith, Hope and Charity**, the rest comes in addition. Ahhh! And put it in Mind and Heart, not just on your lips.
- Toñito! You have given me a beautiful lesson, so it will be brother.

Upright human beings, when they enter into a conversation where something related to the divine appears, express their respect and fear of the sacred, fear because they want their words to never offend the word of God, they understand that the well-conceived word has a meaning. enormous weight in any act, that is why it is important to think and reason before pronouncing it, not to get carried away by the emotions that can drive a harmful word, they cause deep wounds in the soul, their subsequent cure is very difficult, there are no prostheses that can to repair the soul broken by an ill-intentioned word, it is therefore necessary to use beautiful words that reach the ear of the interlocutor, as if it were a symphony of love.

The sensitive source of the human being, must always be filled with the affections of tenderness, affection and compassion, that necessary mercy, empathy and candor, generates in the human being a natural humanitarian attitude towards other human beings, gradually converting their sensitivity in an inescapable strength of own feelings that allow you to rein in your emotions, so that they act in a sensible way and not because of inappropriate impulses, this brake is not to repress or deny it, it is simply a release in time and in the appropriate way , is an early warning to be active in those situations that require greater attention and even any help.

Human faith is closely linked to the belief of a human, in another human, but this depends on their humanitarian acts, this attitude is the verifiable testimony that the human being gives to his divine FAITH, as long as he is a believer in the Source of Superior Energy, that is, **God.**

Following the conversation, the walker asked:

- Toñito, where did you get to this peak?
- Through the same path that you entered, it was not easy to enter this hill, the giant trees and the dense vegetation, did not allow us to visualize a comfortable path, after turning the skirt many times, we made the decision to enter through that way, but what is the irony of life, over time we realized that the minor slope was on the opposite side from where we entered.

  Don't think it took days to reach the top, that took us months, I imagine that you observed the zigzagging of the road, it originated from trying to maintain that beautiful flora and some trees that are very difficult to cut down, it is as if nature itself protected itself for that we did not intervene in it, there were times when our forces were dejected, but our insistence was greater, with time nature itself understood our purpose and today we live together framed within a beautiful harmony.

  When we reached the top for the first time, mounted on a tree, we could not believe our eyes, the visual domain reached the Caribbean Sea, the dynamic city covered by a gray cloud, separated by hills with exuberant vegetation, the impetus of our conquest led us to set booms in the direction of the four cardinal points and thus establish our boundaries, to the north the Caribbean Sea, to the south the freshwater lake, to the east the access road and to the west the legendary trail.

- After settling down. Was there a problem with the authorities?
- Our work was very quiet, the forestry work was carried out from the center of the top outwards, always preserving its natural majesty, the original houses were built with the same wood as a product of deforestation, still young we could carry out hard tasks, for fifteen years of hard work, the plain had already become a town worthy of admiration, when the authorities approached, they had no choice but to support us, because our firm purpose was to carry out a beautiful work for many human beings who were coming to their third age and wanted to live in a dignified way in contact with nature.
- The truth is that you will leave a historical legacy with its own merits and so many people understand that this is the only way to reach Full Happiness, understand that all human beings working together can find the path they are always looking for:

Be happy.

- Comrade, it took more than 25 years of struggle to get to what you see today.

Here is a human example of perfect unity, when everyone needs the correct direction of a safe plan that will benefit a human collective, even though, every human being from the beginning of his earthly existence, has been intimately linked to something that we cannot see or touch. , things that really transcend, cross borders and last over time, due to that natural reason for being, allows him to have the ability to choose and his own conscience makes him differentiate from the rest of the species. This comparison tries to make us see that in order to understand human evolution and the meaning of our existence, **it is essential to think of ourselves as a community of individuals and not as individual persons.**

In this sense, life is extremely important, because otherwise we could not exist, grow, develop links with other living beings, learn, and get to know the world and a host of activities that go beyond mere biological functions.

- Toñito, why did you say gray cloud in the city?
- This cloud is air pollution combined with smoke and polluting particles that float in the atmosphere, they are produced by industrial activity that emits smoke with greenhouse gases and gas emissions from vehicles that use fossil fuels, which which we call carbon dioxide. Such prolonged exposure can damage people's airways.
- I understand that you sought a less polluting environment.
- Correct! The idea is to live the rest of our life in a healthy way, to get away from the effects that cause environmental pollution. Human beings must become aware of not contaminating the air, land and water, these three basic elements are what help us live, imagine breathing impure oxygen, not having fertile land to produce our food and without water with its purity natural. Extravagant and unconscious modernism is leading us to that sad reality.

  Comrade, before this modern madness arrived, our life expectancy was close to a century, in less than seventy years they have reduced it to eight decades, those who manage earthly modernity selfishly live in their glass bubble, perhaps, believing that with money they can buy more hearts to have life. When we express ourselves in this way, many call us socially resentful, if we talk about that, the one that should be resentful is our big house, the mama pacha, how many offenses we have done to her and she, with her nobility and mercy, still gives us life.
- What you are saying, Toñito, makes a deep sense of a great truth.

- We do not want to be selfish, when we decided to undertake this existential struggle, we simply wanted to give an example of union in search of a better life. We are greatly concerned about the life that our descendants are going to have, they will one day become aware of this matter, for the moment our responsibility is to leave a path carved for them, so that they themselves decide which the correct path is.
- Sounds good brother.

The human being during the last two hundred and thirty years, has evolved with the purpose of sharing his wisdom for a healthy world, he has walked through **humanism**, where human values are integrated in search of the greatest possible realism. The discovery of the printing press, maritime routes, the conquest of new continents, among others, generated the entrance of the **renaissance**, where his massive concern was to learn and explore new challenges. The inadequate behavior of the Catholic Church, resulted in a movement of religious leaders who were against the bad practices and abuses that had been occurring within the Catholic churches, the main reformers were Martin Luther and John Calvin.

The industrial revolution brought the use of new technologies applied to mass production, this reality triggered unprecedented changes for societies around the world, changes in agricultural production techniques improved the diet of the population and produced an increase Demographically, in the same way, the steam engine, the mechanical loom and the spinning machine appear, from the economic point of view, it brought as a consequence an increase in mass production, thus creating the development of capitalism with the appearance of large companies . Due to unequal exchanges, in society a division of social classes was formed, the relationship of the individual with his social environment begins to be affected. The predominance of the bourgeoisie as the owner of the means of production brought about the exploitation of labor in industry and impoverished peasants. This reality marked the rise of unionism, socialism, anarchism and communism.

The human being has always sought the way to develop his innate intelligence through his own innovations, these have brought favorable and unfavorable consequences, even when his original thinking has been for the good of humanity, making a very brief historical account of human evolution, and we find the following inventions:

- Archaeological evidence confirms that **the fire** was made intentionally and the method used was rubbing a stick with dry wood, it served to create stone tools, which was the first technological advance.
- Archeology showed that the Sumerians developed **the wheeled** chariot around 3,500 BC. c., as can be seen in the so-called Banner of Ur, a work made with the inlay technique, a typical art of Sumer and Akkad, which consists of embedding stones and other materials in wood. According to recent research, the oldest wooden wheel found so far comes from Ljubljana, Slovenia. It is a wheel from the year 3,200 B.C.
- **The plow** was created around the year 3,500 BC, based on the hoe or shovel, but used together with animal traction, where furrows were already made to place seeds. The peoples of Mesopotamia, located between the Euphrates River and the Tigris River, were the first to use the wheel for the first plows, as demonstrated by the artistic representations of that time.
- **Gunpowder** was invented in China, when the Taoists were trying to create a potion for immortality, the original formula was saltpeter (potassium nitrate), sulfur and coal. After the Mongols conquered China and founded the Yuan Dynasty, they used Chinese military technology in their

attempt to invade Japan, using gunpowder to power their rockets.

- **The Printing** Press was invented by the German Johannes Gutenberg, between the years 1436 and 1450 AD, the device consisted of melting metal letters satisfactorily. In the year 1464 AD, the invention reached Italy and Rome, later it reached France and in the year 1479 AD, Oxford. This innovation multiplied the number of books at low cost and made it possible to expand the number of potential readers, so literacy received a very important boost.
- **The first steam engine** was developed by Eduard Somerset, which he built and patented in 1769 BC, this is defined as an external combustion engine, capable of transforming energy into a certain amount of pressurized water vapor inside a cylinder. , dragging the piston or plunger in all its expansion, thus allowing kinetic or mechanical work to be done.
- **The telegraph** was a device that served to communicate at a distance, it used electricity to send coded messages through the cables. It was Joseph Henry who built the first telegraph in 1829, however, the person who gave it great impetus was the American Samuel Morse, who invented a code that bears his name. News meant money, and the telegraph was the fastest form of long-distance communication.
- The invention of **reinforced concrete** is usually attributed to the builder William Wilkinson, who applied for a patent in 1854 for a system that included iron armor for improving the construction of homes, warehouses and other fire-resistant buildings. The same, roads, bridges, dams, tunnels, industrial works and also maritime works.
- **The telephone** was invented in the year 1854, by the Italian Antonio Meucci, he built it to connect his office

with his bedroom and thus be able to talk with his wife, who was immobilized in bed due to a serious illness.

After more than a century had elapsed, mobile telephony was born in 1973, when the consumer electronics company Motorola launched the first portable cell phone on the market, which was marketed under the name of Motorola DynaTac 8,000X, a artifact weighing almost a kilo. Over time, it has been stylized and evolved until it has become a sheet of glass, silicon and aluminum, a true pocket computer that is also used to talk.

This means of wireless communication through electromagnetic waves shortened distances, improved communication and opened up new possibilities to connect people. This innovation has impacted different areas of modern society; such as globalization, access and distribution of knowledge.

- **The Antibiotic**: The story tells that the British doctor Alexander Fleming, for the year 1928, was working in his laboratory at St. Mary's Hospital in London, on the culture of bacteria, when he went on vacation his samples were covered in a fungus of the Penicillium notatum strain, which destroyed the bacteria. This event gave rise to Penicillin, which was used for the first time in medicine as an antibiotic.

  Alexander Fleming, together with other medical scientists, obtained the Nobel Prize in Medicine in 1945, a more than deserved mention after such a contribution to Humanity.

- **The light bulb** is one of the inventions that revolutionized history, but the authorship of its invention remains controversial. On October 21, 1879, Thomas Alva Edison first showed the electric lamp with a bulb that was on for 48 hours. However, it should be remembered that the German, Heinrich Göbel, had already registered his own incandescent light bulb in the year 1855, long before Thomas A. Edison.

- **The four-stroke internal combustion engine** as we know it today, was developed by the German Nikolaus Otto, who patented it in 1886, based on the studies of the French inventor Alphonse Beau de Rochas in 1862, who in turn was based on Barsanti's internal combustion model.
- **The first aircraft** itself was created by Clément Ader, who on October 9, 1890 managed to take off and fly 50 meters with his Éole. The Éole flight was the first self-propelled flight in the history of humanity, and is considered the start date of aviation in Europe.

  In America, the Wright brothers built a wooden structure with fir and ash and muslin cloth wings, materials with which they made the first airplane. After several failed attempts, the youngest of the brothers, Orville, climbed the Wright Flyer. and on October 17, 1903, they achieved their best-known feat, rising in their first propeller-powered device, the handling of the airplane was the subject of the first patent by the Wright brothers, filed that same year, this happened in Kitty Hawk, Carolina North (USA).
- **The birth of the first computer** was in the year 1936. Where Honrad Zuse created the first computer in history calling it Z1. The Z1 was the first fully programmable computer system. About 10 years later, the transistor was born, which would become an essential part of the electronics that make up a computer.

  A computer is an electronic machine that is designed to perform specific tasks, it processes data to turn it into useful information. In many countries it is known as computer or computer, but all these words refer to the same thing.

- **The Internet** is a network of computers interconnected worldwide in the form of a spider web. It consists of servers (or "nodes") that provide information to millions of people who are connected to each other through telephone and cable networks. It began around the year 1969, when the US Department of Defense developed ARPANET, a computer network created during the Cold War whose objective was to eliminate dependence on a Central Computer, and thus make military communications much less vulnerable.

In the last seventy years, human beings through technology have managed to have the world in their hands, interconnected computers created a communication network that places them in the present time regardless of distance, the space where they are no longer interested, but time to occupy, this reality has created a globalized world, where local connectivity is unified in the context of a supranational instance.

The evolution of the species has always been marked by the fittest, in the same way innovations act, those human societies that do not have the capacity to adapt to this accelerated world of inventions, are slowly moving away from the new geopolitical reorganization that integrates them into the rhythm of the new economy, to the exchange of merchandise, goods and services.

The exponential growth of the liberated market is leaving them without progress, without a uniform culture, an immense unequal gap is being created in terms of their economy, it is paradoxical that the same global lifestyle is promoted, when the differences in the quality of life they are so big, not only between countries, but within each of them.

It is necessary that globalization facilitate the transfer of technology, contribute to promoting innovation and productivity, so that emerging markets exist and thus increase the rate of world economic growth, in order to reduce social inequality as much as possible.

The traveler had observed a well-designed structure where the telematics room worked, inside of which several computers were connected to a communication network, which allowed the technological advancement of the neighboring city.

- ¡Toñito! I was impressed by the communication room. You have thought of everything.
- Of course mate, this tool has helped us a lot, it is used to gather the necessary information that expanded our knowledge, but we are also aware of the terrible damage it can cause to the weak mind of any person, especially infants, there are to be very vigilant in that.
- You say: "Terrible damage", that expression sounds harsh.
- ¡Partner! You and I know that there is Good and Evil, good things are identified with God, while bad things with the Devil, having the world at hand through a computer and a screen is not just anything, the Internet is very useful, but we must be very responsible when we enter that Cyber World.

  Cybernetics deals with controlling communication systems between people and machines, studying and taking advantage of all their common potential, this reality has given rise to artificial intelligence, thus making a machine transcribe the best possible behavior of human reasoning, This well-studied flow of energy is closely linked to control theory and systems theory, that is, cybernetics can control the human mind at any time.

  A character made his approach to the meeting that the traveler had with the inhabitant of that citadel called The Prelude, a community that had been formed with great effort and tenacity, by conscious people who sought a common goal.

- ¡Partner! I present to you my brother Edgar Antonio, here we all call him:

"The Villager".

Chapter II
Social justice.

It was 7:30 in the morning on that Saturday, the traveler sitting in a cafeteria in the city observing the rainy weather that was presenting itself, the gray clouds on the background of the morning sky did not let the sun's rays hit that territory, For the weather to change, the regularity of the city dynamics had dropped considerably, the few passers-by walked with their umbrellas from one side to the other, trying to reach a certain space that for some responsible reason they had assumed.

The walker only had the conviction to continue filling the wait with his well-formed patience, since an appointment had been made with the villager in that place. Four months had elapsed since that first meeting at Pedro Antonio's house, that day marked the beginning of a well-shared friendship, these two characters had many ideals in common, and during very long conversations they talked about humanism, perhaps trying to contribute any ideas that could change the attitude of people regarding their behavior within society.

At that historical moment, technology accelerated social dynamics and nobody wanted to remain anchored in the past, they vehemently tried to be in the front line of combat, regardless of the subsequent consequences, they never realized that within this technological innovation came an implicit irony. On the one hand, it united them socially without looking at distance, however, on the other hand, it separated them in small spaces of human coexistence.

The group of humans that make up humanity, since its origin have sought the way to behave as indicated by its essence, have tried to create cultural values that modulate them in the path of mutual respect and love for the nature that surrounds them. , through communication they have disseminated a scientific development from the perspective of the humanist being, whose integration is not the object of sectarianism or social elites.

The humanist doctrine tries to guarantee the human race cultural parameters based on the discipline, in such a way that knowledge is the fundamental basis to achieve any objective of human interrelation. Being a humanist must have a clear mind to identify the problems that prevent their progress, allows to visualize the errors and analyze it with objective criticism, so that things can fit into everything that has been proposed. Human beings have the right and responsibility to give meaning and shape to their own lives, under the principle of **Ethics** and individual **Freedom**. When the human is empowered by his capacity, he becomes the human being he wants to **BE.**

The villager, after overcoming the obstacles that prevailed due to that rainy climate, finally arrived at the agreed appointment with the traveler, an hour of waiting was enough for his excuse to be comprehensively accepted, the obvious reasons denounced it, while sipping a coffee hot, the conversation began;

- It had been a long time since such stormy weather did not occur in these places.
- I imagine that this is part of climate change.
- Correct partner! Change that is here to stay. Apparently!
- What will be the origin of this change?
- According to what little I have read about it, scientists began to observe this phenomenon at the beginning of the 19th century, when it was first suspected that there were atmospheric changes in the behavior of the climate due to the natural greenhouse effect.
- Natural Greenhouse!
- ¡Correct! This is a natural phenomenon that retains the gases present in the atmosphere as a result of the thermal radiation emitted by the earth's surface after being heated

by the sun, this allows our planet to maintain an adequate temperature for the development of life. Likewise, our big house is protected by a layer that is approximately 20 kilometers thick, thus creating a bubble that acts as a filter against the harmful ultraviolet radiation (UV) produced by the sun, this layer is composed of a triatomic molecule formed by oxygen atoms, which is called Ozone (O_3), is considered a powerful oxidant that reacts quickly with other chemical compounds, it is unstable when found in high concentrations.

- And why the high temperatures?
- The overheating of the earth, due to the increase of solar energy trapped in the atmosphere, which is determined by the gases that have been modified by human activity, in the consumption of non-renewable energy that emits Carbon Oxide (CO_2) , caused by the use of oil, coal and natural gas, this greenhouse effect has generated environmental problems with very sad consequences for humanity, one of which is destroying the **Ozone Layer**, which implies weakening protection against ultraviolet rays that cause skin cancer and cataracts, not to mention that the radiation exposed in the environment is extremely dangerous, because it can cause strong changes in the ecosystems, on which our very lives depend.
- That is very correct brother, all living beings as a whole create a habitat system to have life, its constant flow of energy in dynamic movement presents changes due to factors determined in temperature, light, humidity. the type of soil, the amount of gases and the salinity level of the medium, this leads us to various types of ecosystem, such as: the marine and freshwater ecosystem, in forests, scrublands, grasslands, tundra, deserts and modified landscapes.

When we talk about modified landscapes, on the one hand we must understand all those natural elements that have intervened on the globe to change the environment during its historical evolution, among them: air, water, fire and other compendiums of perceptible transformation, which only They have sought the way to maintain a new stable ecological balance, in many cases it is the transition to a more orderly landscape, these natural actions are found in regions less populated by human beings.

- Totally agree. Now; tell me about the human in those landscape changes.
- The Human! We humans. Since the arrival of the Industrial Revolution, the behavior of people has not been the most sensible in relation to their natural environment, the same demographic growth due to being close to that means of production, led to an incredibly disproportionate population density, where the search for public services were more demanding, the same urban progress began to develop vertical housing solutions with extraordinary dimensions, totally changing its green landscape, for masses of concrete and steel. I have tried to understand this phenomenon of human progress, but I never understood why so many people live in those small spaces.
- I understand what you say. However, we must analyze what they call population density, normally scholars through a census, look for the relationship between a number of people living in a place and the extent of the space they inhabit, the result is expressed in square kilometers.

  We will use artificial intelligence to help us with certain data on population growth in some important cities, generally, these reviews are approximate, however, they provide us with the necessary knowledge to have an idea of this human behavior in contemporary society, within these metropolis we can name the following:

Dhaka: Capital of Bangladesh, located in South Asia.
Approximate population in 2015: 28,395,284 inhabitants.
Territorial Surface: 306.40 km2.
Population Density: 92,674 inhabitants/km2.

New York: City located to the east of the United States of America (USA).
Approximate population in 2022: 22,085,649 inhabitants.
Territorial Surface: 783.80 km2.
Population Density: 28,178 inhabitants/km2.

Mumbai: Economic center of India.
Approximate population in 2020: 18,350,000 inhabitants.
Territorial surface: 603.40 km2.
Population Density: 30,411 inhabitants/km2.

Tokyo: Capital of Japan.
Approximate population in 2021: 13,960,000 inhabitants.
Territorial Surface: 2,194.00 km2.
Population Density: 6,363 inhabitants/km2.

Jakarta: Indonesia.
Approximate population in 2020: 10,560,000 inhabitants.
Territorial surface: 661.50 km2.
Population Density: 15,964 inhabitants/km2.

- ➢ Certainly mate, when we look at these amazing statistics, we can't find words to analyze as far as human sense goes.
- ➢ Correct brother, this simple analysis is the preamble to many questions that have not yet been found answers, from the social point of view.

Contemporary human societies, in recent years have corresponded to the totally accelerated pace that they themselves have caused by their various innovations, in many cases they have forgotten the true essence of human coexistence, where the principles of individual recognition as a being prevail. Social, know and accept the differences that exist in their own characteristics as people, to be able to live covered by the mantle of a healthy harmony that their habitat allows them, in a broader sense, it would be the peaceful and harmonious coexistence of human groups in a same physical space. Humans by nature cannot live alone, even if they try as many times as they want, never in their earthly life will they be able to separate themselves from the womb that conceived them as a being and formed them as human, that eternal relationship brought them into existence and as a human being that exists, needs to interrelate with other human beings, to keep the human species and Humanity alive.

The union of two or more people who decide to live in a single physical space, considered a home and of course, later lead to a harmonious relationship of a home, at that time, can be considered as a fundamental part of a society, likewise, it must be understand that in order to have a fair society, social, family, school, civic and democratic relationships must always proceed within a framework of freedom and justice, of course, with values of reason, trust, respect, loyalty, recognition, tolerance and any fair meaning that feeds that true human coexistence, even when it is necessary to establish norms and laws that allow avoiding or preventing conflicts, as well as punishing offenders in case of being unavoidable, in this sense, coexistence must be framed within the different legal supports and social values.

In the past two decades of the 21st century, individualism with its own characteristics has steadily penetrated contemporary society, humans are vehemently subjected to a spermatozomic struggle, whose preponderant objective is to be in the place of honor that technology itself has imposed, eagerly seeks to satisfy their desires and needs, forgetting the other people who exist in their environment, this sad reality has led them to a glass bubble without doors or windows, where the human value of merciful solidarity can enter.

- Brother! Returning to the human coexistence of these people in those masses of concrete and steel, I wonder what led them to live that way.
- The human species has always evolved looking for areas where there are sufficient natural resources for their own and collective sustenance, at the beginning of time they were satisfied with being next to a river and having nearby land that provided them with food, with the passing Over the centuries, their exponential growth and the modernity created by themselves, forced them to settle in small physical spaces that allowed them to have economic advances, without realizing that the same system was leading them to a lifestyle different from the quality of life, understanding that the lifestyle refers to the particular manifestation of a person in their social environment, which includes their eating habits, personal hygiene, the way of relating socially and with the family, while the quality of life is closely related to the integral well-being, where the individual enjoys good health and physical security, disciplined education in values and principles, decent housing, excellent relationship with their family and the community that surrounds them.
- Totally reasonable, the world is full of conceited people and they are always thinking that material things make them better human beings, leaving behind the greatest value that human beings can have, which is to be spiritual. To be spiritual is to enliven the possibilities of being permeated by the world of God; regardless of the belief that one has of it,

spirituality is always being willing to receive light, strength and goodness from its essence, with which the spirit of the human being can be filled.

- That is how it is brother and that is how it should be, the existence of the Human Being, in the earthly world.
- At times I understand the socially materialistic world, its development has led people to live with a certain comfort, but there are others that exaggerate the opportunities that life has given them.

The human being by nature is endowed with a tangible body that leads him through life and this, in turn, is conceived by a brain where the mind becomes the main director that commands the existential senses of the thinking human, the same, within That body and mind, there is the spirit that directs them in the earthly world, although its essence manifests itself in an intangible way, every human being knows that it exists.

The spirit goes beyond any dogma that society may impose, its intrinsic manifestation in people will always be guided by the Divine Faith that it has and conceives in its mind, depending on its actions, the human being can feel a state of emotional, psychological and social well-being, which will determine their ability to function and deal with the problems of human interrelation in earthly existence. In a broader sense, it regularly implies the intention to experience special states of well-being in solidarity, empathy, charity, mercy and any humble gesture in the positive of its natural essence.

Spirituality, today more than ever, has the obligation to provide the human being with the necessary elements for the resignification of life, of history, of the present, and from there the consolidation of God's project in life; a project that is renewed and expanded from the dimensions of the spirit.

There are some research studies that link spiritual well-being with physical well-being. Spiritual well-being can be a comfort and can give you strength to face life's challenges. Some people find that taking care of the spirit seems to be as healing as the medicine itself.

Likewise, spiritual health implies reflecting on our beliefs, achieving a state of well-being in harmony and balance with: being charitable, being compassionate, learning to forgive and asking for forgiveness, knowing how to reconcile, spreading hope, sharing hospitality, giving appreciation and affection. , valuing gratitude, practicing humility and standing up for justice, these practices will give us the ability to function optimally as a human being and have the energy and vitality to be highly productive and successful in any area of our lives.

Spiritual healing is also obtained by expressing and listening to humble testimonies. The testimony that is expressed in a spirit of repentance, of gratitude for divine providence and in accordance with divine guidance, is also a powerful remedy to alleviate the anguish and worries of our hearts and in the same way, cleanses the conscience in the impure acts committed blindly of reason.

As for the material, it is an element that can be transformed and as a whole it can have a real, virtual or abstract nature, in the same way, they can be used to manufacture or build something, they are found directly in nature and indirectly when its elements of vegetable or organic origin are transformed.

But when we talk about materialism, we must point out its historical origin in the development of the production of material goods necessary for human existence, whose main force determines the social life of humanity and conditions the transition from one social regime to another that is why it is that no society can exist without producing material goods.

The ancient belief thinks that human nature and natural nature are material because they can be seen, touched and felt, therefore it is real, this unfortunate condition has led humans to be more competitive, manipulative and selfish, causing consequences that have affected common well-being, social relationships and therefore the quality of life, when people are dedicated to pursuing wealth and material possessions, they tend to be less satisfied and experience fewer positive emotions.

Materialistic people who focus their way of life on promotions obsessed with money and possessions, which have been imposed by the consumer society, unfortunately, spend their entire lives thinking about what they own and what they appear to have, now , focusing on intrinsic values and not on material things, favors personal well-being, not continuing to think that money can buy happiness and only using it as another marketing instrument for what can be bought, this leads to improving our health mentally, so as not to fall into the obsessive desire to accumulate money and wealth, which can lead a person to suffer from crematomanía and like all other manias, it is difficult to treat.

People who suffer from this pathology respond to a profile that is highly marked by personal interest and the desire for social and professional recognition.

Only dialectical materialism allows solving in a scientific way the problem of the relationship between thought and being, clarifying the most general laws of nature linked to society, its vision as a whole covers a complex chain of natural phenomena, To obtain favorable results, it is essential to feed knowledge, since it allows the development of critical thinking, in such a way that a pedagogical action can germinate from that source, product of the consequent relationship between theory and practice.

- Buddy, one day on the internet, without realizing it I came to a page that talked about the rich and famous, like all curious, I began to investigate that world extraordinarily outside the normal context of life, imagine that a single person identified with any amount of billions of dollars, a figure that my mind really could not analyze in depth, I carried out a single mathematical exercise and the result was surprising, I formed a normal family of five people: husband, wife and three descendants, dividing that astronomical figure between Those people, even leading a lifestyle at its best, would have to live 500 years to spend that fortune.

Comrade, that seemed to me a vulgar exaggeration of human vanity and I am not saying it out of envy of that reality, in the end that is everyone's problem in this world, it just seemed to me something that I did not understand or understand in the context of the inequality that there is in humanity.

- Inequality! Social inequality. Sad reality that we live in a world full of opportunities and that only few people have been able to take advantage of.

  Social inequality has always existed, but in these times it has been extremely significant, due to the same development that some advanced societies have had and the imposition of certain ideologies or values of some human beings on others, understanding them as the discriminatory treatment they exert on Those who are less favored economically, socially or morally, this distressing situation is due to an inadequate distribution of opportunities and respect for access to goods and services, which is based on various cultural or social reasons, however, many do believing that this type of action is human in nature, of course it is not a form of justice and neither is it divine punishment. Likewise, we must understand that social inequalities are not the same in some societies, due to their exclusive class linked to socioeconomic issues and others considering issues of race, religion, sexual orientation, etc.

- Correct brother, but we must not forget that this unequal classification is closely linked to the following reasons for segregation:

  Economic position: Probably the most common form of social inequality, is anchored in the economic capacity of the individual or the class to which he belongs, thus separating the world from the rich, the middle class and the poor, obviously to the detriment those who occupy the lower rungs. Those who are lower on the scale have less access to goods and services, to political representation, to symbolic and cultural visibility, as well as to study and even adequate food.

  Depending on how far apart these social strata are, we can talk about caste societies, in which climbing to the upper rungs is practically impossible.

  Religion: Religious struggles are as old as man, and in many modern societies they still constitute a factor of inequality between human groups, reserving power and opportunities for those who profess a certain Faith, thus condemning those who profess otherwise. , often referring to them as "infidels" or "heretics."

  Gender: This is discrimination based on biological sex (as in the case of women) or sexual orientation (as in the case of the LGBT community), which reserves the commanding and most favored positions for heterosexual men (especially if are white) and marginalizes those who do not subscribe to a certain traditional ordering of sexual or erotic roles.

  Ethnicity: Racial discrimination grants a superior position to certain races or ethnic groups, subjugating others to their will by considering them “inferior” or “different”, and thus denying them access to goods or even fundamental rights, such as life. Some of the great massacres and genocides in history are based on this type of discrimination.

Ideology: In this case it is about political discrimination, that is, the inequality of opportunities and goods between those who adhere to a political doctrine and those who do not, or who oppose them. This is what happens in totalitarian governments or dictatorships, for example.

- Certainly brother! Likewise, we must not forget its causes and consequences in the 21st century. Social inequality does not have a single cause, but is a consequence of the way in which our history as a species has passed. The French thinker Jean-Jacques Rousseau, reflected on the origin of inequality among human beings and assured that the origin of this was found in the social state, that is, that man is not born in inequality, but rather acquires it by begin to compare yourself with your peers and see the way they live.

  The study of primitive societies has shown that they were much more egalitarian societies in the distribution of work and benefits, but somewhere in the Neolithic period a process of hierarchization and construction of the State began, which implied the distribution of labor and social division, something that would reach its highest peak with the invention of slavery and the exploitation of man by man.

  Social inequality has very concrete consequences and very contrary to the harmonious development of nations or humanity. The perpetuation of poverty, the strengthening of resentment and the need for revolutions or violent conflicts are just some of them, since the discomfort of being stuck in immovable social strata often leads to depression or anger in oppressed communities.

  On the other hand, the oppressed never fully develop their potential, since the resources necessary for it are being used by others, which causes an incalculable loss of human potential hidden in those trenches. And poverty, far from being a simple evil, is the source of numerous difficulties that are extremely difficult to combat: the risk to health, the increase in crime, class hatred, the deterioration of politics, etc.

In these times the human societies that as a whole make up Humanity, should take the necessary actions to break the paradigms that have been created in social inequality, whose separation today is extremely abysmal, in this sense, there is a need to seek the necessary elements to ensure that true Social Justice is imposed.

Although it may seem a complex issue because it touches on the interests of equality, who's right to opportunities is closely linked to the correct and fair distribution of goods within society, in order to achieve the Common Well-being of the human being. Undoubtedly, this necessary reaction will lead human beings to the understanding of building a more equitable and less unequal society, to have a world guided by the word of Divine Justice.

When we talk about social equality, we are not referring to a forced equality of the social and economic status of the members of a society, but the guarantee that everyone, without exclusion, can fulfill themselves in the exercise of their human rights, civil, political, social and economic, which includes equality before the law and equal opportunity.

Likewise, when we refer to equal opportunities, as its name indicates, we are pointing to a society that guarantees a social stratum, where individuals develop their human potential, despite being born poor, in addition to ensuring that citizens have the same opportunities to demonstrate the innate talent that they carry within their existential being, in such a way that they can share it with other social classes.

To achieve the true value of Justice, it is necessary to understand it as a virtue of the human being, who only seeks a clear and powerful reasoning, so that each individual receives what corresponds to him by right, regardless of his social condition, that dignified treatment is the recognition and total respect for their human rights, therefore, puts each individual in the place they deserve, without discrimination and respecting their individual liberties. Consequently, every society must be based on Justice, unfair acts violate the rights of the person, taking away their freedom. It is important that individuals and society as a whole, fight against the injustices that can occur in the social, work, and family, among many others.

From the philosophical point of view, throughout history, many thinkers have based the theme of Justice, as follows:

Socrates: The knowledge of what is fair is enough to act as it is due.

Plato: Justice is the harmony of society.

Aristotle: Justice is proportional equality, which means giving each what corresponds to him and has to do with his needs, contributions to society and his own merits.

Saint Thomas Aquinas: Justice is a natural law that is, granted by God.

Baruch Spinoza: It is just the one who has a constant desire to give each one what is his, and unjust the one who strives to make what belongs to another his own.

Gottfried Leibniz: When the individual puts himself in the place of the other, he can be in the true point of view to judge what is fair and what is not.

At the moment that human beings have a clear awareness of the straight path of life, it will logically form a Healthy and Just society, with the purpose of making the balance fall in a positive way, in such a way that all its members in harmony can definitively move away the terrible evil of Egoism, to return to the nature of the common good, linked to **Peace and Love.**

Chapter III

The Naked Soul.

The conversation that the traveler and the provincial had for hours became more cordial at every moment, they changed places so that time would not be implacable and their actions could stop that interesting conversation, the trust that had been generated between these two characters , allowed one of them to ask a very direct, daring and perhaps even suspicious question;

- Edgar Antonio! Would you be willing to tell me about your personal life?
- Wow brother! That proposal caught me off guard. What would be the purpose?
- Some time ago, I thought about writing my own autograph. I propose you join this beautiful project.

- You try to tell me that you are going to write a book about your personal life. I see it as a very serious responsibility. What would be the intention of talking about yourself?
- The idea is to leave written in my own words to my future descendants who was I? Perhaps divine providence will not give me the opportunity to see them personally.
- You make me remember, brother, something I read about the steps that the human being must take in this world, with more or less words, said something like this: "Human beings, in order to give meaning to their earthly life, must not leave that the world pass through it, leaving intangible traces, but rather, on the contrary, to pass through the world leaving tangible traces with much love, which are demonstrated by: Planting a Tree, having at least one Descendant and writing a Book ". I have already fulfilled these three maxims, I only need to write a Book about my own earthly experience, but I see it as a very daring challenge.
- Brother! Cheer up! The time has come for you!

For a person writing a book on any subject is a way to grow and feel good about themselves, it helps a lot in research and exploration of the sensitive world in a positive way, it creates mental dynamics to better organize the time of their earthly life, but above all things, he leaves reflected in letters written on a sheet of paper, the reality of his own emotional feelings, that release is also a way of communicating an understanding repressed in his thoughts and that was never expressed, in the same way, he could considered **as a courageous way of stripping the soul of its own Being.**

- The soul of the human being is considered as the intangible part that inhabits the body that gives us the ability to think and feel, is capable of giving life to the organism and is the immaterial essence that defines the individual and humanity. Baring the soul is showing yourself as you are, showing the most important thing about you, your feelings, your desires, your dreams, your virtues and strengths, your fears and your fears.

- When a person's soul is caressed with seductive words, unsuspected emotions are immediately ignited, which may be hidden in the deepest atoms of their human feelings, an act begins that goes beyond the human body, a focused connection is created in the faces of his personality and when he touches his heart, it has nothing to do with time, because, at that moment, it can fill you more than another person in a year.
- Taking advantage of this opportunity that his friend the walker gave him, the provincial sipping a hot chocolate and breathing deeply, he took on the challenge with integrity and sanity, courage and daring, he knew that his words were headed for a sheet of paper and he did not want to that its naked phrases, perhaps in the not too distant future, could possibly be read by people alluding to a feeling susceptible to indescribable emotions to the reasoning of any human race, in that sense, its content should be very restrained and framed in the synderesis of reasoning, so that there was a good understanding.
- My mother, Merari del Carmen, said that I was born in a public hospital in a town in the plains, called Valle de La Pascua, located in the Guárico State. At one in the afternoon of that February 20, Nineteen Fifty-Seven, she already had me on her chest, giving me affection, affection and providing me with nutrition with the milk that flowed from her breasts.

  She said that my father Pedro Antonio came over and she excitedly told him with words full of a sublime feeling: "Here is your birthday present".

  Well, my father that same day I was born, he was turning thirty-four years old, from that marital union, I was the first offspring, they identified me with the name Edgar Antonio, I suppose Antonio arose from my father, the Edgar, I never knew why.

He told me that he had not turned three years old, when they moved to a central town in the Anzoátegui State, called Cantaura, in that town my grandfather José Ruperto on his father's side, was in charge of registering me as a civil person born in Venezuela.

I would have been maybe five years old, when my mind began to be filled with reliable information, I remember that it was in a town called Anaco, which was only fifteen kilometers from Cantaura, the house where my life really began, was attached to the house of My grandmother Rosa Celestina on my mother's side, the sector was called Pueblo Nuevo and as its name indicates, it was still in development and lacked many public services, however, they were gradually incorporated.

I must confess to you brother, that my mind was marked by poverty, I had not turned eight years old, when I already had a sister named Elvira del Valle and three brothers: Pedro Antonio, Orlando José and Alexis Rafael, despite having a modest home, our nutrition was very scarce, however, my sister, my brothers and I never stopped eating something before going to bed, all on a double mattress that my grandmother had given to my mother.

Poverty has been defined as a human condition characterized by the continuous or chronic deprivation of the resources, capacity, options, security and power necessary to enjoy an adequate standard of living and other civil, cultural, economic, political and social, understanding it in the same way, that it is not only an economic question; It is a multidimensional phenomenon that includes the lack of both income and basic skills to live with dignity, and when talking about extreme poverty, it is defined as a combination of low income, lack of human development and social exclusion.

People living in poverty face enormous obstacles to exercising their economic, social and cultural rights, the consequences of which are interrelated and mutually reinforcing, such as hazardous working conditions, unsanitary housing, lack of food nutritional status, unequal access to justice, lack of political power and limited access to health care, which in turn prevent them from realizing their rights and perpetuate their poverty. People submerged in extreme poverty live in a vicious circle of impotence, stigmatization, discrimination, exclusion and material deprivation that feed one another, until they lose their Social Freedom.

Currently the world has been characterized by an unprecedented level of economic, technological and financial resources development, this has caused a moral scandal where millions of people live in extreme poverty, to eradicate this evil, it is not only a moral duty, but also a legal obligation, framed in international human rights regulations, whose preponderance is to ensure all public policies that affect people living in a state of inhuman poverty.

- The origin of my father and mother, dates back to the beginning of the 20th century, my father was a man who at an early age, life led him to drag the chains of misfortune, he lost his mother Virginia Elvira (My Grandmother), when she was barely For seven years, he developed his existence through the Guanipa savannahs, until he learned the profession of driving trucks with five-axle traction. His work as a transporter forced him to part with his family for long and anguishing days.

  My mother came from the eastern mountains between the States of Sucre and Anzoátegui, in the same way she traveled the paths of adversity, being the eldest of a sister and six brothers, at the age of fourteen she lost her father Pedro Maria (My Grandfather). My grandmother and she were in charge of raising their family, the job she really learned was to take care of the home to perfection, later assuming the same responsibility with my father.

My childhood was developed in an environment surrounded by many economic hardships, with a father who was a tireless fighter, he sacrificed practically his entire life behind the wheel, to provide the necessary support for the family and also for those who were not family, within his being. implicit duty of solidarity towards the human being in need, the trade she learned, due to her well-instilled responsibility, at times did not allow her to give her family the deserved human warmth, in the same way, my mother carried on her shoulders the great commitment to educate and feed their offspring.

That was the culture that I learned when I was young and which was already walking since my ancestors, the man provides and the woman disposes.

Anaco in those days, was a town in full oil and gas development, many North American service companies installed their work infrastructure and urban fields to live, so my human development was closely linked to that Anglo-Saxon culture.

In the Venezuela of the 20th century, a very important element in energy emerged from its bowels, many countries already called it Oil, and this reality totally changed the economic context of its inhabitants, at that time there was no real mentality of what was happening within its sphere and less beyond the national sphere. When the experts arrived with their technology to explore the deposits, they immediately realized the great wealth that lay beneath the subsoil and with all their intentions, they raised negotiations that tipped the balance to only one side.

This economic impact that was presented transformed the country from an agricultural income to an oil company, whose profound consequences led to paternalism and state clientelism. There is no doubt that the oil bombing, under the broad condition of the term, practically shapes economic, political, social, and institutional and, perhaps, cultural of the country. As a phenomenon, it has gone through different phases during the Venezuelan oil era, but today it is in one of its most critical stages. The understanding of this event and its implications is extremely limited, both in the political system and in the general population; therefore, addressing the problem from a multidisciplinary point of view would allow it to be analyzed and understood in a broader dimension.

Today more than ever we must underline the phrase of Alberto Arvelo Torrealba, which articulated, Dr. Arturo Uslar Pietri, on July 14, 1936, which I quote: "Sow the Oil".

- “It is urgent to take advantage of the transitory wealth of the current destructive economy, to create the healthy, broad and coordinated bases for the future progressive economy, which will be our true act of independence. It is necessary to extract the greatest income from the mines in order to fully invest it in aid, facilities and stimuli to agriculture, breeding and national industries. That instead of oil being a curse, that it has to turn us into a parasitic and useless people, it is the fortunate situation that allows, with its sudden wealth, to accelerate the productive evolution of the Venezuelan people in exceptional conditions.”

- ¡Brother! Even having all those economic difficulties, my childhood was very happy, I was lucky with my street freedom, of course, with the sectorial limit that my own mother imposed on me, and be careful if I broke that agreement!, so as not to lose that freedom, in a disciplined manner he complied with his rule. In that limited space there were two warehouses and their owners, to attract all of us who ran shopping errands, created the barn game, which consisted of depositing corn grains in a container for the purchase that was made, then the accumulated grains, they exchanged it for gifts, which could be: metras, top or trinkets. Of course, that created a fair and healthy competition, today I understand the message of those winemakers:

¡Become a man by working for what you want!

- Message with intelligent action.
- Correct brother, as for the traditional games, we used to fly parrots that we built ourselves, many stayed on the electricity cables, others on the trees and those that were cut with blades in mid-flight, and these were almost never found. Playing wooden top, the truth is that I wasn't very good, but playing metras I was a tiger, I managed to accumulate I don't remember how much, I have an anecdote about them:

  It turns out that in those same days, they gave me a trip to Caracas as a prize, for having finished sixth grade with excellent grades. Before traveling, jealous of my goals, I kept them in a metal container and buried them in a part attached to the home, without anyone knowing of course, I got a bigger surprise when I returned, my dad had built a laundry room in that place. That was the first great sadness of my life.
- It is not for less brother, you lost a very big trophy won in good fight.
- At that moment I said to myself "I am going to recover what I lost", but it could not, times had changed, my stage as a

primary student at the Simón Bolívar School, I was falling behind, my white coat, I was changing it for a complete khaki uniform, which was the requirement of the new Creation Lyceum, that's what they called it. That is, brother, my existential world was changing in all aspects.

Human beings, during their biological evolution and social development, must have the same treatment and recognition as a subject of law, in order to get involved in matters that concern them, assuming the responsibilities inherent to the fulfillment of their duties granted by the gradual exercise of the citizenship.

It is necessary to understand the stages of the biological development of the individual, they as humans are not the property of any other human, they were born free and will be free forever, as a member of a family and a community, their rights and responsibilities must be adapted to the different stages of its integral development, therefore, the character must be assumed as a person in development, capable of progressively assuming responsibilities with the power to give an opinion and express with individual freedom, their concerns within the society to which they belong.

- In the change from school to high school, the extreme poverty of my home was slowly moving away, we all already had our own bed to sleep in, my mother no longer sent me to buy kerosene for the kitchen and the old refrigerator, we began to drink water cold from a fridge powered by electricity, there were chairs to sit down to eat at a table as a family, our feet said goodbye to the espadrilles, my mother proud with her radio to listen to soap operas and my father had bought a used brand car Ford, Failane 500 model, white and blue color, year 1958.

  This reality made me feel very proud of them and with the same impetus, I began to attend classes at the high school, the change was remarkable, there was no longer a single teacher who educated us, now, they were teachers who taught us classes in different subjects, we all had to adapt to the way of being and acting of each one of them, that process of adaptability was not easy, brother, but the same dynamics of camaraderie created a very beautiful spirit of joy, many schoolmates found ourselves in that room high school student

High school student! When I heard that word for the first time, I understood what it was like to climb one more step in the lights of knowledge, at that precise moment, my thoughts went flying towards the university, I just had to continue climbing the steps that came, with a lot of strength and will.

Brother, I confess that this was one of the most beautiful stages of my life. I don't know how yours was.

- Totally agree with you, I also experienced not only the changes from one school campus to another, but also the natural biological changes of the human being and the new social relations of a world characterized by a heterogeneous gender, located in a single physical space, the which should be framed in the healthy disciplined orientation of values and principles, coming from a stable and functional home, today I thank divine providence for having given me that blessed opportunity.
- Good brother, in my case it was something different, the Liceo Creación, was the first public high school for secondary education in the sector, the other high school was on the opposite side of the city, because it was the only one, our student population was Made up of all social strata of the community and even of different nationalities, including: Americans, Canadians and Germans, remember that Anaco housed many foreign companies. Now, this student diversity made a very big social difference, sometimes the same

paradigms planted by the punishing society stigmatized innocent young people of that perverse reality that led them to drop out, I remember a friend who was in our group, very intelligent and vivacious, he depended on a family with very limited financial resources, well, he only lasted the first year, but you know one thing, brother, a few years later I saw him again, a medical graduate.

The social label that the punishing society of **"I CAN'T"** had imposed on him was taken from him I don't know where.

- Excellent brother! How wonderful about that valuable friend. The worst thing that can happen to the human being is to fill his mind with that malevolent phrase **of I CAN'T!**
- ¡Correct! I also believe that in order to remove all the taboos and paradigms planted in our minds by the punishing society, it is extremely urgent to use all the resources that modern technology allows us, to find the true path of knowing oneself, today, the The same dynamics of time is leaving behind the certain reason for thinking, thought is the only way to find and value one's own human existence.

Knowledge as an essential part of the thinking human, is currently an unavoidable duty of necessary food, its adequate proportionality will be the engine of a new social reorganization, in order to heal the wounds that we have caused for millennia, not only to our species, but also to all the species that inhabit our invaluable nature and to the Superior Energy Source that directs us.

Filling our memory with positive, healthy and healthy knowledge implies real awareness of our personality traits, behavior patterns, emotional state, self-esteem, beliefs, values, needs, objectives, preferences and social identity of oneself, this knowledge allows us to regulate our attitudes, solve problems effectively and make the right decisions, in the same way, we learn to identify the extent of our capabilities and limitations.

Finding yourself, it may seem like a very tangled path of life, in that walk we must learn to control and manage our emotions, for this, it is very important to know the definitions of each one of them, in order to give it the right value to situations and circumstances that arise in human relations, this purpose can change a positive relevant fact to a negative one or vice versa, behold, its vital importance. As an example we can name **Anger,** this emotion when carried away by improper impulses, people generally make mistakes that are very difficult to repair, this perverse manifestation could be considered a living act of the devil himself.

When the human being is subjected to this difficult test, the moment can be handled without the need for confrontation, without falling into prejudice and observing the situation presented with great aplomb, this will allow him to think carefully about the correct response that the counterpart deserves, at that moment. the thinking human could even be considered from a philosophical point of view, a true stoic, let's not forget that the wars that have existed in humanity have been due to the confrontation of two sides, no one fights alone and if they do, it would actually be a true madman or crazy.

People within society, when they reach the crystalline consciousness of being Human, at that precise moment begins the stage of valuing oneself, without letting themselves be dragged by the undue valuation of egocentrism, their human behavior demonstrates innate solidarity as a natural being created, to give love to all existential things in the universe. It is important to understand in the same way that every existential cycle has an end of useful life, therefore, the sooner the human consecrates his human existence within humanity, and without a doubt his worthy valuation will be that of a **Human Being.**

- Brother! When I told you about that wonderful path of being a high school student, it is because all the human emotions stored in our hearts are awakened, personal feelings manifest spontaneously with the undeniable divine purity, we are beings with a true spirit of solidarity, trust, respect and loyalty to All of our fellow students, the truth is that this stage, considered as a student community, could be socially valued as unique, of course, it is also the stage where we know the sadness produced by disappointments and failures, these attitudes make the hidden atoms of reason and understanding, to place us on the right path.

- Reason definitely leads the human being to think and reflect, in such a way that our mind can understand the sensitive relationships of the human being's fair understanding. Following this guide will lead us to value the true concepts of Love and Friendship.
- Love and friendship, how beautiful it sounds.
- I imagine that in your high school life you handled everything related to Love and Friendship well.
- You have touched a very sensitive point of sentimental emotions, to bare my soul in that world full of obfuscated romanticism, I must clarify to you the importance of a healthy and healthy orientation in the paths of life, even more so, when the paths that appear they are governed by different biological, social and cultural changes. With this I do not seek an excuse for the mistakes made, I assume them with all responsibility and the person who reads these lines, I humbly ask for human understanding.

The academic record of my studies in the first and second year of high school, was qualified excellently, when I started studying the third year, I already had sixteen years of life, at that moment my heart was impacted by emotional feelings towards the female sex , I began to discover the wonderful world of love, my hormones woke up uncontrollably and acted like that, without realizing I was falling into the merciless pit of lust, this reality brought as a negative consequence, abruptly lowering my academic record, however Seeing my mother sad because of me, I immediately redirected my path and gave her with satisfaction, having saved the school year.

My father and my mother, as a reward for this beautiful act, sent me to study in Caracas, the reason that had a significant influence in making that decision was to separate myself from that world that they possibly saw as the fundamental cause of the mistake made. During the process of my mental maturity, I sought to redeem my ignoble acts in the eyes of **God.**

Redemption as a human act, seeks God's forgiveness, for all the errors or sins committed in the earthly world, that manifestation from the soul, leads to Peace and a rain of spiritual blessings sent from The Superior Energy Source.

Human Beings who keep their Soul clean from: Pride, Laziness, Gluttony, Greed, Lust, Anger and Envy, will have no problems when the Parousia (Second Coming of Christ) arrives, because their spirit will be strengthened to enter the **God's Kingdom.**

Chapter IV

The Solidarity.

Santiago de León de Caracas, was founded by Don Diego de Losada in the year 1567, ten years later it acquired the status of

Administrative Capital of the Province of Venezuela, for that date it had a population of approximately 2,000 inhabitants, for the year 1810, Its population was estimated at approximately 42,000 inhabitants and for the year 1973, Caracas being the Capital of Venezuela, its territorial conformation was made up of the Metropolitan District of Caracas, whose Parishes were: Libertador, Baruta, El Hatillo, Chacao and Sucre, its total population, over 2,200,000 people.

- In the last quarter of 1973, he was already installed in the apartment of an aunt on the father's side, which was located on the Intercommoned Avenue of El Valle. I remember that four years ago, I had spent a vacation in the same sector, another aunt lived nearby, but in a colonial-style house, two hundred meters away was the square, the church, and a cinema, that is, a town within a city in progress When I wanted to visit that aunt, they took me to an apartment, unbridled modernity had disappeared from all the houses, to give way to vertical developments, when exchanging words with her, there was a phrase that had a great impact on me, which said: **" How I miss my beautiful garden".**
  Behind those words, there was a deep human feeling, a woman over seventy years old, whose movement through life had not been easy for her, since her first child had been born special to her, when she was barely eighteen years old. What are the things in life, brother, she died at the age of ninety-two, and a month later, her first offspring left, perhaps, at some point in her prayers, she had asked God for it.
- As you are saying and I believe so, definitely, that divine connection had been fed, with all the strength of love that a mother's heart has, possibly, she knew that no one was going to give her that same love.

Here is one of the importance of the Prelude community, which you have wisely managed to develop, your aunt missing that garden, it could have meant a call from nature, so that he could once again have contact with his natural essence as a human, that relationship of land, water and air, is never lost, even more so, when life announces its decline, it is not the same to live in masses of concrete, than in a flowery field by nature itself. With wise words you said it one day:

"The Prelude is an open-air nursing home".

Old age comes to the life of the human being, playing a preponderant role of lights in knowledge, no matter what has repressed his memory, the important thing is that he always has something to say to those who want to hear it, his words are like a book open, their gray hair, their soft hands and their tender gaze, deserve deep respect, physical and verbal abuse towards them, we could consider them and include them as an eighth sin to the seven that already exist, to make it legal, before earthly laws and spiritual, before the Divine laws.

An old man not only transmits experiences and wisdom, but also with much affection and affection, gives wise advice and emotional support, so that families always remain United and sheltered under the Sacred Mantle of Love.

In this sense, the family and society, in recognition of their valuable contributions, is the supreme and inexorable duty, to provide them with all the substantial and necessary support, so that their old age receives dignified treatment, so that when their transcendence inevitably arrives, they feel in his heart the Spiritual Peace that every human being yearns for, to be in the Kingdom of Heaven.

- Divine providence did not give me the opportunity to personally meet my grandmother Virginia Elvira on the father's side and my grandfather Pedro Maria on the mother's side, today I say to the four winds with deep respect, affection and pride, thank you for carrying your genes inside of my being and allow me to honor them with all my heart, because people who knew them, expressed beautiful and wonderful words, the referenced quotes filled my memory with all the sublime that can exist in a human being, when it is their turn to represent a family with dignity and Also to which I belong.

- Fair value and recognition deserve all those people who manage to reach old age, both those who left, those who are and those who will come, because at the end of everything, it is not easy to earn the Title of **Grandmother or Grandfather.**
- Returning to my stay in Caracas, I continued my high school studies at the José Avalos High School, it was very close to where I lived, that student meeting was not easy, the mere fact of coming from the province meant for them coming from the mountains, the A punishing society had imposed the phrase "Caracas is Caracas, the rest is mountains and snakes", that label was marked with the mere fact of speaking, even so, student camaraderie always prevails, although my group was reduced to only one companion and one co-worker.

  This reality made me turn my feelings to the land where I was trained, for me at that time there was no comparison of one space with another, but circumstances marked it that way, however, I was filled with strength and courage, to enter a process of adaptation necessary.

  Forty-five days later, a student revolt broke out, my classmate and classmate, understanding my inexperience in this type of situation, saw my desperation and protected me under a ladder, the room was filled with thick smoke that did not allow me to breathe, tears came out of my eyes immediately, they gave me a handkerchief impregnated with vinegar, which allowed me to ease my breathing a bit, the short time that the situation lasted, for me it seemed like an eternity. After having lived that first experience, I asked many questions and received few answers, I only understood that it was a social discontent, due to bad political decisions.

From that moment I began to investigate the meaning of social discontent.

Human beings by nature were subjected to a process of socialization, due to their characteristics and needs, it was essential for them to create societies of human coexistence, these should be oriented to a set of activities that are associated with group decision-making, in order to to make a healthy distribution of natural resources.

In this sense, politics emerges as a science that deals with the activity carried out by a government and the organization of human societies, especially states. Likewise, it can be considered as an activity of those who govern or aspire to govern the affairs that affect society or a country.

Generally, people who freely constitute themselves in groups with political will, seek Social Justice as their objective, always based on the affinity of criteria, interests and aspirations for political action, in order to strengthen the social weaknesses that affect the individual as a life, its basic orientation is circumscribed to requests for changes in administrative management of public goods delivered to a government.

The reason for any political movement should not be limited only to gaining power, but rather have a fair awareness of the reason for which it was granted, because if we speak of Social Justice, the right path must be oriented to protect the rights essentials of the Human Being, such as: life, the right to a healthy diet, health, education, the right to decent housing, the right to a job to start a family, which allow the development of person, for their economic and social growth.

Undoubtedly, without economic growth, there is no social life, even more so when contemporary times demand it, therefore, all political movements, no matter how different they may be in their ideological thought, it is of the utmost importance to understand that the political power granted, does not it is to benefit a few, quite the contrary, since by benefiting the majority, few or nothing would be the oppressed, these political acts are positive, without detaching themselves from a healthy economy with a progressive sense, of course, which would be the tool necessary for the attainment of **a Humanity filled with great Wealth and Spiritual Nobility.**

Always understanding that the eminently human person is not only identified by his wealth in material goods, but by Being A Dignified and Noble Human Being.

- I remember one afternoon sitting at the viewpoint of the cota mil, with some cousins trained in a rebel sector of the capital called January 23, watching how the city itself denounced its marked social difference in the human habitat, to the east, housing estates with houses with red roofs, vertical buildings with modern architecture and several shopping centers with neon lights, to the west, a hill eaten away by people desperate to have a place to live with their families. Seeing such an immense social difference, my blind innocence only asked: Why do Human Beings live in such an inhuman way?

"Cousin! To understand and comprehend this sad reality, it is necessary to study the great thinkers of history who have tried, in one way or another, to shorten that abysmal gap that separates us. Soon I am going to lend you some books so that you can cultivate your mind that will help you it will allow us to analyze and glimpse what Social Justice is all about."

I confess to you, brother, that since that day I began to read a lot of literature on the matter, the truth is that I still do not understand that mysterious world of human behavior, so many struggles and wars that have existed in humanity, always using Social Justice as a banner to achieve power and what they have done in the end is to create a social abyss, where humans can no longer give themselves a human hug, this despondent scenario cannot be called **Humanity.**

Another experience that marked my coexistence in the capital, was going to the eastern park with other cousins, Sunday was chosen by many people to socialize in direct contact with nature, in that place I observed entire families recreating their infants, the same people performing sport and body exercises, but I also paid attention to many young women who walked from one place to another, most of them were not even 20 years old, they were all very beautiful and with spectacular bodies, the question came up with the spontaneity of lightning Where did so many beautiful women come from?

"Cousin, those are maids who work in the family home, they all come from the province and today they give them the day off, so they can share with their friends."

Time later taught me that every human being tries to locate himself in the space of opportunities, of course, this happens when the opportunity is not in its place of origin, this reality is the consequence of the rural exodus to a place that allow you to grow as an individual, the unfortunate thing about the matter is that this human action obeys when there is a central power without public policies, directed especially at strengthening the means of production, in the ideal spaces of natural resources and worst of all, is that They call province, the spaces where the true wealth of a country is, not only in human resources, but also in the natural.

- Brother! What you are saying deeply touches the human mentality, people who inhabit any physical space and do not have the opportunity to nurture their minds in the lights of knowledge, will always live walking the dark path of ignorance, a terrible evil that takes away from them the right of human beings to live in full freedom, imagine a country.
- Correct brother, our geographical space in the world, was blessed by divine providence, we have all the necessary natural resources, so that we all enjoy an extraordinary quality of life. Unfortunately, somewhere along the way, someone closed the door so that our mentality could not visualize the beautiful world of life.

The first thing that a human being, located in a certain geographical space, seeks is to carefully observe the existing natural resources in their environment, starting with water and land, this will allow them to create a source of food, once this fundamental biological need has been met. , everything else comes in addition.

All humanity is aware of this simple reasoning, however, there is a part of it that does not seem to understand this imminent priority, any people that has food sovereignty will give them enough time to think about the consequent social needs, let us not forget that a Malnourished people lose the ability to think, so that this terrible evil does not happen in society, it is necessary to cultivate knowledge towards a progressive mentality, in such a way that other natural resources serve to create a stable source of economic income, in order to satisfy the insufficiencies of good living.

Many countries without natural resources have demonstrated it and many countries with natural resources have not demonstrated it. The difference between one and the other lies in the **Mentality.**

The human mentality can coexist in a world of multifactorial pressures, but it itself creates the nuances of a healthy and healthy experience, for that it counts on all the natural resources of the environment, if these resources are managed with human criteria for the common good, the they will contribute to competitiveness through innovation standards and environmental technology, in order to improve the productivity of economic actors, attract investment and promote new sectors in the creation of products necessary for society, this productive activity must be carried out in a sustained manner, to avoid the depletion of resources that may directly affect the economic development of the same society.

Once the human mentality understands and comprehends that natural resources will make it possible to satisfy the necessary requirements of: food, clothing, housing, education, health and other goods, it must also think about leaving guarantees of well-being for future generations, for this it is The intervention of the economy is necessary as a key piece in progress, with a broad and comprehensive vision that allows combining different approaches and facing the current problems of humanity, caused by an arbitrariness between the human and the non-human, for which it must be impose strict discipline as a fundamental element in its exercise.

- How long have you lived in Caracas?
- Just over a year, enough time to have learned to live the customs of the capital, the academic experience was very nutritious, I must also admit that it awakened in me the value that living as a human being means, I say this because I carefully observed two faces of human coexistence, one of them very fighting to overcome the adversities of day to day, the other with a better quality of life, perhaps thinking about how to climb one more rung, in the scale of their social stratum.

  This sad reality made my mind fly towards the thinkers of social antagonism, in them I could find the answer to grow as a person, within society and shorten the distance that separated them.
- That seems excellent to me, you made a wise decision.

The human by nature is endowed with the beautiful gift of Solidarity, it manifests itself on many occasions and even spontaneously, unfortunately, society in its evolution has tried to overshadow it and even, within its selfish world, has wanted to disappear it , at this point, the thinking human begins to develop methods of coexistence so that she becomes stronger, this task has not been easy, since ancient times there have been humans who diverted the purpose of life in common, towards individual vanity, thus fulfilling their animality of the fittest, to be above the least favored, today, in contemporary times, the dispute persists.

In this sense, the thinking human is called to return to the sensible world, to reject the unjust acts of social life, the practice of its noble causes will feed the spirit of solidarity, it is of the utmost importance to combine charity with social conscience, reason special that must exist, to change the negative inserted in the human heart, for the positive, today and forever.

Let me summarize some of what some people in Ancient Greece thought:

"In the understanding that the truth is in each one of the people, regardless of their social condition, it is necessary for the person to have knowledge of what is good, beautiful and just, so that the end of their acts is framed by their very reason for Social justice. That person who cannot distinguish with reason the idea of the good and who cannot apply himself correctly to his search, not according to appearance but according to its essence, will not have knowledge of the good in itself, nor of any good thing, and if he reaches a image of this, it will be by mere opinion, not by the essence and by not finding the true nature of human existence, it would be entering into nothingness and nothingness is unthinkable, because it does not exist, because what is, simply is, to be It is necessary to think about what is, since it is possible to be, while it is not possible for nothing to be, therefore, this will never be imposed, that they find things that are not. In conclusion: Nothing exists, if not all good things in the sensible world, we have different opinions, but when knowing the reason, it is transcended to the intelligible world, the main idea of this world is that of good, as clear as the sun that illuminates the earth."

The Human Being, once he understands and comprehends the sensible world of good, will begin in the same way to grant time, its fundamental value as a virtue of life, which will allow glorifying all actions of good being disciplined at work, punctuality, honesty and study, in order to do everything related to those objectives, of course, all these acts will be to learn to give, without receiving anything in return, which will lead us to be well with our social environment, which It is the same to say, the community welfare state, slowly plowing all this way with significant Hope, Faith and

Charity, divine providence will tone all that effort with the good of having the most sacred thing that the Human Being seeks, **Peace, Love and Happiness.**

When people decide to work for the common good of the human being, they must necessarily know the value of what is good, beautiful and just, in this way it would be easier for them to fight against the terrible evils of human thought, understanding that its errors are bad. Habits that distort the interpretation of a reality, this weakness results in difficulties in social relationships.

- In this sense, we must learn to manage our mind, so as not to fall into the following errors:
- Interprets others and events in absolute terms, without nuances or middle ground.
- From a specific event, generalize all situations.
- Only process the negative aspects of an event or person, without attending to other characteristics or positive aspects that are also taking place.
- Take full responsibility for a negative event, believe that anything negative that happens or is said is because of it.
- Believing guess, by the fact of having thought, the thought or intention of others.
- Evaluate in an overestimating or underestimating way, a fact, event or attitude of others.
- Thinking that the worst can happen at any time.
- Interpreting facts based on how I feel, instead of interpreting objective reality.
- Evaluate the facts as "should be" without contextualizing.
- Evaluate and classify in absolute terms, instead of attending to the concrete fact.
- Attributing responsibility for their problems to others or assuming the blame for the problems of others.
- Interpret facts in a way that fits what you think.

- Believing that everything can be controlled, believing that nothing can be controlled, and believing that others are in control.
- Believing that if he is not right in everything, he loses his worth, this leads him to interpret the environment and others as a threat, if they do not agree with me, I will constantly try to prove that my opinion is correct.
- Maintain the belief that sacrifice is the measure of a reward and if you don't, you can be punished. This distortion usually leads to a constant need to meet the expectations of others, without taking into account their own needs, thus creating fear of consequences.

Once the distortions that predominate in our minds are focused, conscious work can be done to readjust thought or what is known as "cognitive restructuring", which will positively influence more adaptive behaviors and reactions.

The thought schemes of each person jump automatically, trying to exercise control over a certain environment, in order to reduce the feeling of uncertainty and existing anguish. This can often lead to the confirmation of a hypothesis such as a "self-fulfilling prophecy", maintaining and making thought schemes even more rigid, for example, by personalizing and doing a thought reading of a social situation generated by anxiety, The same circumstances can create situations of fear of rejection, a scenario that can be present throughout the social experience, such as a negative subjection: "I'm sure they think that what I've said is nonsense, that's why no one comments anything" , this will lead to the rest of the evening remaining silent and fewer and fewer people will take it into account, thus confirming the belief that others tend to reject it, when in reality it is the attitude and body language that is making people believe. Others the interest that they prefer to be alone.

Learning to adjust our thinking, trying not to cloud it with our main fears and insecurities, in addition to giving us a more objective vision, will help us feel good about our environment and those around us, and of course, with ourselves.

Basically, to be a social fighter you have to be sensitive, disgusted by injustices, whoever endorses noble causes is in a position to correctly interpret solidarity and put it into practice. The combination of sensitivity and social conscience, leads the individual to a commitment to activities that can contribute to the sensible path of justice, to the reason that can justify the existing engine of change in the negative, for positive actions for the future, the subject he feels obligated, driven to work so that the changes that society requires for the collective good materialize.

The actions of a social fighter, responds to the fact that they perceive in their intimate feelings a terrible situation of injustice, they do not avoid the duty to place themselves on the side of the oppressed, as a consequence of iniquity resulting from an unfair economic and social order, which rests on the shoulders of inequality of opportunity.

The person of firm convictions, committed to social changes, feels the duty to carry out tasks in favor of a community, fulfills the liberating mission that has been imposed for a sincere cause with those who demand Justice.

It is proven that whoever seeks the liberation of the human being from all social oppression fights for love towards others, trying at all times to build a new order; institute a new society; establish an atmosphere of fraternal coexistence; create the environment where love flourishes and not hate, peace and not war, integration and not discrimination.

He who adheres to social transformations, commits himself to their achievements; to push with passion to achieve them; vehemently carry out as many missions as they are in charge of, and do them with height; and to behave magnanimously before the adversary, he seeks an environment that represents the joy of a community, he is aware that he is an actor in a position to be willing to remain belligerent, to be a warrior against everything that expresses backwardness and injustice.

The sensitivity of ideas when they are embraced and materialized for the common good, achieve the true enjoyment of full happiness full of joy, on the contrary, indifference to the suffering of others, is a demonstration of insensitivity, coldness and lack of compassion.

Whoever decides to walk the path of leading the new dawn of a community, is because they feel they are a human being, prepared for sacrifice, because wanting to break the chains that oppress the great majority, has as contenders those who benefit from the oppressive system. , and their conscious and unconscious allies.

Optimism must be accompanied by a good state of mind, so that social changes are the reason for their existence and lead them to be, openly contrary to everything that is related to hopelessness and disappointment, because negativity and despondency only generate pessimism. , which is not a stimulus for victory.

Proof of being coherent in his thought and preaching, is one who understands the negative reality where he lives and works to transform it, to change it to positive and thus make it suitable for a good material and spiritual life, for the majority of those who make up the society.

The protagonist modifier of the established order, must have a humble and simple behavior, demonstrate his work with sincere and honest joy, as something that is enjoyed; with easy-going actions, stripped of vanity, without being ceremonious, you must understand and comprehend in the same way, that joviality is of the essence of those who are in love with the development of tasks in order to ensure that changes occur for the social progress of the community.

Within human societies, there are also scoundrels, who only need to disguise themselves with an honest mask in the morning, an honorable mask in the afternoon and a beautiful mask of a social fighter, at night.

Transfiguring himself to distort his person has made it possible for the homeless man to walk around in the suit of a tin moralist, pretending to be a supporter of the fight against social ills, when in truth he is nothing more than a dissident, deserter, defector, transitory renegade of corruption. Human.

The scoundrel who wants to ascend to where honest women and men have reached with dignity, must be lowered, thus ensuring that he does not climb up, does not settle where he does not deserve to be. **In the home of the pure of heart, the dirty of feelings should not stay.**

Chapter V

The Good and the Evil.

In the 1970s, the hydrocarbons industry grew stronger due to high oil prices, this allowed Venezuela a fairly substantial economic entry and expanded to other regions of the continent, unfortunately, this reality only lasted for a short time and instability began to undermine the foundations of social life.

Likewise, in this decade there was a great boom in the television and film industry, giving rise to an accentuated production of Venezuelan novels and films. In the year 1969, North America opened up to the world as the country with the most social freedoms, its advanced technology this was allowed, among other events, two historical events marked humanity considerably, the trip to the Moon and the Woodstock Festival, this three-day event of Peace, Music and Love, housed in a single physical space, more than half a million people, the impressive musical waves filled the minds of many Latin Americans, silently invading the already established culture, however, within this area a melodious romanticism was awakening that has prevailed for more than five decades.

- So brother, you came back to Anaco.
- That's right, I returned to my homeland, to the town that was no longer a town, the same oil dynamics was turning it into a city, I observed a very important demographic growth, directed towards the four cardinal points, the north marked an orderly development, the perceptible The difference was possibly due to the criteria used by people with greater capacity to extend how to manage empty spaces, to turn them into urban planning, while in the south, the development was totally different, perhaps the same desperation of people to have a physical space on land Abandoned by their owners, it led to an unplanned occupation, of course, since there was no authority, anarchy began to do its excessive work. That unfortunate scenario made my mind see again the two faces of a social coexistence, the favored and the disadvantaged of the opportunities provided by the means of production.
- Unfortunate brother, very unfortunate. These are the circumstances that many politicians take advantage of to gain followers, using these human needs, they begin to make all kinds of promises, which in the end are not fulfilled, as they should be attended to.
- ¡Correct! Seeing this sad reality, sitting with some friends in the town's Plaza Bolívar, a debate began on how to help stop this overflowing noise, suddenly the idea of intervening through a theater group arose, this way could allow us to

carry the message that we wanted to the competent authorities, it was an indirect way of knocking on the doors of human sensibility.

- What a nice idea they came up with! A play through the dialogue between characters, allows to reach many hearts.
- Correct brother that was our idea, to put together a work that represented unfavorable situations within social coexistence, including inequality, the value of having opportunities in the means of production and community public services, among other important things.
- Tell me. How did it go?
- To develop the idea, we needed a physical space, we all came to the conclusion of going to the Ateneo de Anaco that was the most suitable cultural site, of course, our project was very well received, the receptivity of the members of the board was in a very pleasant way, until they realized the central point of our plan.
- What was the plan?
- A critical theater group called "Because". We gave it that name, due to multiple questions that arose due to bad social policies that needed firm answers, in consideration of many people from the town who were walking towards the abyss of poverty, in a place that was generating a lot of economic wealth, morally ours. My mind did not understand that disconsolate context, therefore it was necessary to intervene in any way, for that reason the revolutionary spirit awoke in us, in this sense, and we were filled with courage to face this situation without looking at the future consequences.
- What were the consequences?
- We staged a play called "Christmas", in which the reasons for a social reality that needed a prompt response were implicit, many of them were addressed, others required more time, I must confess that our work was felt with that

single play, which we took to many corners of the city, without realizing we were touching the interests of a society in economic progress managed by few hands, that is, we swam in deep waters like fish, but ignorant of the sharks that were nearby.

- I don't understand that hard expression. Explain it to me!
- A geographical space that generates a lot of economic wealth due to its natural resources, generally there are people who try to seize them, to achieve this objective, they focus on obtaining the facilities that political power can provide them, in such a way that their investments can be protected from any eventuality contrary to their interests.
- Apparently brother, our humble intention to change was putting these people on alert, so they made a master move to weaken the momentum we had. In this step of life, it is important to understand and understand that all our actions were motivated by emotions without proper experience and guidance in this regard.
- What was that master move?
- There was a fellow high school student who approached us in a spontaneous and kind way, on many occasions he agreed with our way of thinking, little by little he gained our trust, one day he suddenly expressed an understanding with us, well, There was a teacher at the high school who was very tough in her pedagogical practice, her way of acting was incomprehensible, her treatment of the students did not correspond to the true way of educating, for this reason she had to be protested by us, we all agreed that this was the case. Outside.

  Brother, that same morning we moved to look for tires, a chain and a padlock, to close the main access gate to the high school, the same colleague with a borrowed truck made everything very easy, our youthful impetus did not allow us to see what we had to see . The time came and the protest began its actions, we all got a bigger surprise, on the other side of the fence, there was the comrade who invited us to the protest defending the student campus, shouting any insult against us, all of us perplexed, we had no words to say , only in silence we could maintain loyalty to ourselves.

- ¡Wow! I am surprised by the vulgar way of doing an unfair act.
- That sad reality marked my life forever, the high school authorities approached us in a very pedagogical way, in a private meeting we received the necessary guidance to decline our attitude, and they made us understand the little time left to graduate from high school. the republic, the director of the high school with wise words made us understand something very beautiful, I quote: "Boys, you have a long way to go to understand life, do not vote out the window for the title that will open up a range of opportunities for you at the university, to that tomorrow they will be professionals serving society and their country". So we did.
- And the theater group?
- After having known the face of betrayal, we gave ourselves a time of reflection, without realizing it, time took care that each one looked for the corresponding path for his life. For my part, I went to work in a rubber farm, to help with household expenses.
- Definitely brother, when the owners of **power** perceive that they are touching their interests, they look for a way to destroy any form that they consider threatening

Nature, within its own evolutionary system, has created the necessary sources to maintain balance, however, there are certain exogenous elements that intervene so that this does not happen, which is why on many occasions it has been necessary to sacrifice those things that do not allow maintain the balance in a firm way, these actions are caused by the same power of nature, in this sense, human existence as the main witness, must preserve natural environments and change the relationship of exploitation with the environment, this would be the key point, to maintain a healthy Humanity.

The genesis of the formation of human groups has shown that many humans seek the supremacy of power over other humans, these sad circumstances have led them to iniquitous confrontations that have only left misfortune and desolation on our big house.

In the 21st century, it is necessary for societies to reorganize their way of thinking in relation to power, contemporary times demand a radical change in the assessment of the human as a Human Being, it is not possible to continue manipulating the mind of a human, to make it do what another human wants and likes, true power is not in whoever exercises it, but in whoever accepts it, this reality feeds the powerful source of energy that every human has implicitly from its origin, therefore, new societies should definitively uproot all the taboos and paradigms planted by anachronistic societies, with the firm purpose of valuing their own human existence. To reach this important state of the human mind, it is necessary for thought to learn to manage emotions, whose appreciations of external events, current or past, must be evaluated in order to obtain an emotional response that transcends the certain way of living.

- How was it in the rubber band?
- My work consisted of procurement and collection, during my work practice two important events happened, one was the move of my family to the city of San José de Guanipa (El Tigrito) and the other was meeting a beautiful girl who later loved her. I did my wife.
- Brother! You're telling me that you married as a teenager.
- The circumstance that arose at that moment in my life was not easy, the mere fact of being left without my original

family practically freed me from all responsibility towards them and from them to me, understanding this truth in the good sense of the word. word, because human beings are never released from the responsibility they have towards their family, in this context, it was as if divine providence was telling me: "Now you are a lonely man who must learn the ways of life", it is tell; At that moment I felt that the decisions of my life were mine alone, any step I took was under my sole and exclusive responsibility, but the most endowed with beauty was that inside my backpack I carried a whole world of illusions blessed by my mother. And my dad, which were framed in values and principles that I never lost.

- What a beautiful brother, but tell me, how was that marriage?
- Leave the pranks brother. It would not be easy for me to bare my soul in that context.
- Why?
- Out of respect.
- Who?
- To life.
- ¡Correct! It is your life and we are talking about it, behind your eyes I see a clean soul.

Human beings during their existence have always traced their life path, the same path has given them the opportunity to understand and understand why they exist, the great scholars of the origin of life, although they have had their theoretical controversies of evolution and creation. , they have shown that there are only two paths to choose, at this crossroads is where the human finds himself face to face with the two faces that will mark his life forever: the path of Good, sensitive to Love and the path of Evil, Defined by Hate, the first is filled with knowledge to defeat ignorance and illuminate the correct path forever, the second tries to keep humans submerged in the dark ignorance, so that they never reach the true feeling of **Love.**

During this process of human existence, the same knowledge takes him to the intangible world, that unknown world that makes him think and feel natural emotions, but he still does not know where they come from. Time clears up this dilemma, he begins to understand that Within his material body there is a spirit fed by the soul, at that moment for him, a spiritual world is born that in the same way is fed by Faith, likewise, the human has understood that he is immersed in a field full of energy, This in turn is motorized by vibrations that can reach a higher energy source, a source that in turn feeds all those human vibrations that walk guided by positive love. That Higher Energy Source only has one name: **God.**

In this context, the human body would be the physical part, the soul would reflect everything related to emotional feelings and the spirit would be the one that lives closely linked to the spiritual world, so the function of the spirit is to bring all its energy closer to the Superior Energy Source, so that in the same way it is rewarded in its existential Being and the function of the soul, it would be its positive expression manifested in feelings of Faith, endowed with understanding and freedom.

This reality tries to give meaning to human life, that is, while the body is a healthy conductor of a pure or purified soul in the vicissitudes of life by liberation in the eyes of God, undoubtedly, the strengthened spirit would live sheltered by glory from the Superior Energy Source, that is; **God.**

- ¡Brother! Thank you for that beautiful expression towards me, not every human being has the ability to look at the clean soul of another human being, although there are always humans who try to place that black point that stains the beautiful picture of life.
- Personally, I don't think I deserve such recognition.

- Why?
- All human beings have committed sins, some directly and others indirectly, it is a lie that they tell their social environment everything, there will always be those who are taken to the grave, however, those who have had a deep relationship With the God of your belief, in your act of sincere and honest spiritual acceptance, I am sure that your sins, confessed in that divine intimacy, have been forgiven, so that your conscience strengthens the redeemed spirit before God.
- Is that how you feel brother?
- ¡Of course! That is why I have the courage and courage to tell you about my private life without any pretense, even so, I will try to summarize the facts and circumstances of a not very graceful existence, for which I ask for your respect and deep understanding.
- I will do so brother.
- After three years of having known Margarita Mercedes, there was an event that was not understood by her mother, even though I had behaved like an honest gentleman, her incomprehension led me to demonstrate my honor with a civil marriage, after accepting and understanding my good intentions, a month later came the ecclesiastical marriage.
  ¡Dude! I invite you to put your imagination to flight, in it you will see a seventeen-year-old girl and a twenty-two-year-old boy, without the proper experience and preparation, facing a demanding and punishing society; However, we did so, the road was not easy, I must confess that many external obstacles disturbed the true understanding of that honest relationship, we did not have the firm orientation that gave us the weapons to face all those changes, even so, two years After our marriage, the youthful impetus led us to conceive our first child, after three years a daughter came and the following year another daughter. I have always thanked my

God for having rewarded us with those three human beings: Beautiful, Strong, Healthy and Intelligent.

- So, the family you formed was: your wife, a son and two daughters?
- No brother, there were three more human beings.
- How was that?
- I want to ask you for a lot of understanding in this regard, two factors entered into the marital union that we did not know how to wield, on the one hand the impetuous young man who had not learned to handle emotions overflowing with masculine passion and on the other hand, a young woman empowered by the ghost of jealousy caused by the ignoble acts of a blind husband, this sad reality led us to have a dysfunctional home, perhaps we were selfish in not seeking the necessary help to stabilize the relationship, on the other hand, a truth that may sound ironic may sound He never let us see the madness of our acts, the mere fact of not having lived our certain youth, led us to be separated many times, perhaps, the purpose was to continue living without ties, what we ourselves tied, that reality without giving ourselves account, it was leading us to a relationship that fell into the vicious circle of life, today we get together, tomorrow we separate.
- It is very sad to live like this.
- Of course brother, those are the consequences of assuming such a serious responsibility and without being prepared. The truth is that there was a lot of distance between the two and this allowed loneliness to enter, we know that loneliness is not a good adviser and it leads us to walk through the world that one believes is right, of course, by not knowing how to handle it, mistakes will and they come, some make your mind mature and others strengthen your spirit, at the end of the whole process, the important thing is to have assimilated the negative and positive

circumstances, which allow you to have a vigorous conscience.

- In this present of life, how do you feel your conscience?
- Strengthened! I feel like a fulfilled man, I have no material goods to leave to life, what I do have is a spiritual fortune closely related to the God of my belief, for a long time I have not let anyone disturb that divine relationship, I have a lot to recognize and thank my Lord: Jesus Christ.
- Thanks and Recognition! Those are words that weigh immensely.
- Sure brother! Within my gratitude is having rewarded me with four daughters and two sons, I confess that I was not an exemplary father, providential circumstances did not allow it, but as I would have liked, with the maturity that I have, to share with my offspring useful ideas for life ; however, I feel deeply proud, because they have been warriors of human existence, with resilience they have forged a totally firm character, which has allowed them to be advanced people in a world that is more demanding every day, in that sense, my Recognition to God, because that is how it has been and will continue to be, until the last breath of my earthly soul.
- Brother, why do you say you were not an exemplary father?
- The knowledge of life has taught me that being a direct partner in the procreation of human beings, which is a very great responsibility that our God has entrusted to a man and a woman, because it is not only the maternal conception, but bring them into the world in the healthiest way possible, as well as form it with all the love that a mother and father can have.

  That was the moment that made me reflect as a father, since my wife and I, even though we were two disoriented young people, could have grown up with our offspring, whose firm purpose was to start the true family project within a stable home, which It had to be focused on the responsibility of providing them with values and principles in a coherent way, guaranteeing their healthy survival, creating an environment of respect and love, taking advantage of all opportunities to communicate positively, providing them with a well-disciplined education based on spiritual knowledge of free choice. , teach them that their body must be kept very healthy, because within it moves a soul and a spirit, a spirit that one day will transcend to the kingdom of heaven and thus be with the God that their Faith has conceived, teach them that they came free and with a life purpose, a purpose for which they must always fight and walk, of course, permanently covered with the sacred mantle of the freedom, which will allow them to find the true meaning of human existence.

Here, brother, where I assume the responsibility of not having been the father that they expected.

- I congratulate you brother.

Not everyone bares their soul in such a sincere and honest way.

- Before I say goodbye, I am going to tell you something very beautiful that happened in my life, one of the books I wrote, which is called "Sueños de una Campesina", in those pages I wrote the story of a fifteen-year-old peasant girl who lived a romance fleeting summer with a young city dweller, as a result of that overflowing passion a girl was born, her mother sacrificed 25 years to train her as a true medical professional, her father never knew that this girl existed, after having spent almost forty years, Father and Daughter met in the United States.

  Two years after finishing that story, my personal life was extraordinarily impacted by the following event, 36 years ago I had an affair with a girl whom I called "comet of my loves", this was due to her sporadic appearance, I never knew where she lived Five years later, he appeared with a photo of a beautiful girl, we agreed to meet the girl on a walk in the park, that day never came.

After 35 years, that girl was kind enough to look for her father, he appeared in the United States, and today we have a very nice relationship. Her name is Arelis Patricia and she has two beautiful children.

- Brother! That's amazing. How does what you wrote match reality?
- I call it Positive Energy Vibrations, sent by the Higher Energy Source!
- Correct brother, that beautiful reality only has one name: **¡GOD!**

levels" this was due to her anorexic appearance, I never knew where she lived ... years later, he approached with a group of ... [illegible] we agreed to take the girl on a walk in the park ... [illegible]

After 25 years, that girl was ... [illegible] ... in the United States, and today we have ... [illegible] ... Her name is ... [illegible]

[illegible]

www.ingramcontent.com/pod-product-compliance
Lightning Source LLC
LaVergne TN
LVHW050331160826
845677LV00014B/3591

* 9 7 9 8 3 6 6 3 2 2 1 2 6 *